Who shot
Queen Victoria?

To Gabrielle Rowly-Conwy

First published in 1996 by Franklin Watts
96 Leonard Street, London EC2A 4RH

Franklin Watts Australia
14 Mars Road
Lane Cove
NSW 2006

Series editor: Paula Borton
Designer: Sally Boothroyd

A CIP catalogue record for this book
is available from the British Library.

ISBN 0 7496 2210 5
Dewey Classification 941.081

Printed in Great Britain

Who shot Queen Victoria?

A History Mystery

by

TERRY DEARY

Illustrations by Linda Birch

W
FRANKLIN WATTS
LONDON • NEW YORK • SYDNEY

Contents

Introduction

History is full of mysteries. Stories are passed down through the years and most of us believe them simply because they are written in books. But sometimes the writers get it wrong! History writers have been known to . . .

· make mistakes
· exaggerate
· invent 'facts'
· leave out important facts
· tell whopping great lies

This makes your job of understanding the past very tricky.

What is the truth? Who is telling it?

When a detective sets out to discover the truth he may have to solve a mystery. He must ask questions and work out who is lying and who is telling the truth. In this book that's just what you have to do. Become a history detective.

You will be given some fascinating facts mixed with some fascinating lies. Sort them out and solve the mystery. This *History Mystery* is arranged in three parts . . .

Part One

To make the mystery more enjoyable to read, it has been re-told in the form of a story. Imagine yourself in the shoes of two young detectives. Travel back in time and see how they uncover the evidence.

Part Two

To help you understand the world in which the mystery is set, there is then a selection of facts about the people of those days and their lives. Some of these facts will help you solve the mystery, others are simply fascinating facts on their own.

Part Three

Finally the story ends with the characters reaching their own 'solution' to the problem. You might not agree with their solution – some historians would certainly disagree! But remember . . . it is *a* solution, not *the* solution. In history there is hardly ever such a thing as *the one* right answer. That's why history is so strange and irritating and enjoyable and infuriating. History is a mystery . . . and *that's* a fact!

Part One

The story of an Assassin

1

London – 29 May 1842
The girl was the saddest thing I'd seen in all my life. Her red hair hung in ringlets around her thin and sickly face. Her blue eyes were ringed with grey pools of tiredness in a white face spattered with freckles. "Please sir," she said to the gentleman next to me, "have you just a few coppers? Mother died a year ago today. I only want to buy some flowers for her grave."

The man in the black frock coat reached into his trouser pocket and found some pennies. He pushed them into her hand without quite being able to look her in the eye. The girl looked up at his whiskered face. Her voice was cracking as she said, "May God bless you, is the prayer of your unhappy but true friend!"

I knew I was next. I only had sixpence. My fare on the railway home. She took a step towards me, her eyes looked up to heaven, she staggered suddenly on the cobbles and fell softly to the ground at my feet. There was a puddle of mud in the gutter and a pile of horse droppings a little to the left. Luckily she fell between them and her faded black dress, poor but with spotless lace, stayed unmarked.

I wasn't sure what to do. I was on my way home from school when I had seen the crowd lining the pavements of Constitution Hill. "What's happening?" I'd asked a gentleman in a black frock coat. "Victoria," he said gruffly. "The young queen and Prince Albert usually ride this way each day. The people like to see them, don't you know?"

I was in no hurry to go home. Mister Allison had kept me behind after school for untidy work. I tried to explain that it was untidy because my hand was hurting where he'd smashed a ruler across my knuckles for an ink smudge. He didn't listen. He never did. Sometimes I thought he must be deaf. Anyway, I'd missed the early train so I decided I might as well wait to see if Queen Victoria drove past. I was interested in carriages – father had a small brougham and I wanted to see how the royal carriage compared.

Now I found myself with a red-haired, ringleted girl lying lifeless at my feet and I groaned. With Mr Allison's beatings, and now this, it was turning out to be a bad day.

While I was still wondering what to do, a man stepped forward. He wore a silk top hat, neatly brushed but a little worn around the seams. His black coat was going shiny at the elbows but he seemed to have covered the bare threads with black ink so the worn patches didn't show. Clearly a man who liked to keep up appearances but who had fallen upon hard times.

"Let me look at the child," he cried to the crowd that was gathering around her. "I was once a doctor," he said. I guessed he must be about forty years old. His side whiskers were red, but the rest of his hair was going grey.

The doctor raised the girl by the shoulders and pulled her gently towards the kerb where he sat her down and waved a bottle of smelling salts under her nose. He checked her pulse and lifted an eyelid to check for signs of life. He looked up at the crowd. "A simple case of starvation," he said. "The child has clearly eaten nothing for days."

The girl's pitiful eyes gazed up at him. "No, sir, I haven't. I've been saving for some flowers for my mother's grave."

The man helped her to her feet, pulled out a leather pouch and opened it. There were a few pennies inside. He held it open. "I haven't much, my child," he said, "but what I do have is yours."

There was a sighing and muttering from the crowd. A woman in a green crinoline dress stepped forward and pushed a shilling into the man's pouch. One by one others dropped money into the purse. Even the gentleman in the black frock coat gave some, though he'd just given her a handful of coppers.

One man hung back. A young man with a rough brown coat of shoddy material and badly fitting trousers. He was too busy looking towards the top of Constitution Hill with a fixed stare. His eyes were red-rimmed and his face unshaven.

As the girl was helped to her feet and the doctor disappeared into the crowd, I turned to see what the rough young man was looking at. A landau carriage had appeared and was trotting briskly down towards us. Uniformed soldiers rode on either side and three people sat inside it. A plump young woman in a deep blue dress sat next to a thin man about the same age in a uniform. I guessed they were the Prince Albert and Queen Victoria. The other woman must have been her lady-in-waiting.

What happened next was the most dramatic thing that has ever happened in my life – maybe in anyone's life! I can see those pictures in my brain as clearly as if they were photographs . . . except I see the picture in *colour*, and no one can take photographs in colour!

The carriage rushes towards me.
The queen is looking away from me and waving at someone on the far side of the road.
The prince is looking straight at me.
Suddenly his mouth falls open and he gives a cry.
The prince throws an arm around the queen and pulls her head down.
The queen gasps and laughs.
I hear a clicking sound in my ear as the draught from the carriage pulls at my cap.
I turn to see what the prince was looking at so horrified.
I see the rough young man in the brown coat lowering his arm.
He is holding a pistol.
He mutters, "Fool that I was not to fire!" then slips backwards into the crowd.

At first I thought I'd imagined it. But the girl with the red ringlets was staring after the gunman. "Oh, John, you fool!" she said. At first I thought she was talking to me.

"What?" I asked.

She shook her head impatiently. "Nothing," she snapped and hurried after the man.

I turned to the old man in the frock coat. "Did you see that?"

He was shaking his head and blinking rapidly. "How extraordinary!" he muttered. He turned and walked up Constitution Hill.

"Did you see it?" I asked him again. No one else in the crowd had noticed anything. They were chatting happily and moving away.

"How extraordinary!" the old man repeated and crossed the road. I had to decide what to do. The girl's red hair was bobbing through a mass of people on the pavement and I caught a glimpse of her every now and then. The old man was a witness – but *he* couldn't help me to catch the assassin.

The girl, on the other hand, seemed to have set off in pursuit of the man with the gun. If I followed *her* then it might lead me to *him*. I hurried after her, my school bag banging against my thigh, and as the crowds thinned I was able to slow to a walk. I didn't know where the chase would end and, curiously, I never gave it a thought at the time. I certainly didn't think about what I'd do if I ever came face to face with the man with the gun.

Perhaps I imagined I'd find the nearest policeman. Father told me that every town was copying London's example now and employing policemen to safeguard the streets. But, he said, the London police, formed by Sir Robert Peel, were the best.

The girl began to head for Oxford Street where the carriages of rich people stopped at the fine shops. Little boys swept mud and horse droppings from road crossings and earned halfpenny tips.

The girl stopped at a corner, had a quick word with a crossing sweeper. The boy shook his mop of greasy hair in answer to her question. Her shoulders drooped a little. She looked carefully around. I guessed she'd lost the gunman. I stepped behind a carriage and hoped that she didn't see me. When I peered round the wheel I saw she was heading east, but more slowly this time.

Once or twice she stopped and stared into the windows of the grand Oxford Street shops. Perhaps she was dreaming of the fine hats displayed there; hats that a poor girl would never own. "How foolish," I thought.

In fact she was not looking *into* the windows. She was looking at the *reflections* there. She was making sure that I was following her.

There was only one foolish person there . . . and it wasn't the girl.

2

The pavements were crowded with shoppers while the roads were filled with carriages of all types, donkey carts and horses. Coachmen shouted at horses and at each other, costers with their barrows swore at everyone and a small flock of sheep bleated and pushed their way past protesting people. The noise and the smell were overpowering.

Still, I was pleased that I kept the bobbing red head in sight as it headed for Holborn. At last the crowds thinned as we left the rich shops behind and headed for the city's poorer parts.

The tall houses and shop fronts were older and dirtier here, but I had no idea what lay behind them. The girl stopped at the entrance to an alleyway, paused just long enough for me to see where she had gone, then vanished down it.

I hurried after her and was so excited by the chase it took me a while to realise what I was going into. The alleys here were a maze of paths so narrow that the houses overhung them and blotted out the evening light.

Open sewers ran down the middle of the alleys and half-clothed children crawled in the slime and the stench. The houses had small windows, many broken and blocked with wood or rags. The shops here spread their cheap clothes in lice-ridden piles outside the doors. Men and women picked at the poor bundles and haggled with the shopkeepers.

On some corners beggars sat and clutched at my legs as I hurried past. Their sores and skinny bodies were pitiful but I only had my train fare. But worst of all were the eyes. From doorways and windows and gutters there were eyes everywhere. Watching me. Men stood in groups, watching silently as I hurried past, but their eyes took in every detail of my school clothes. Small gangs of boys began to follow me through the maze. Still the girl hurried on, pausing to speak to someone every now and then.

Now I realised I was lost. I had no idea of the way I had come and I had to keep going forward through the twisting, darkening lanes, through the crowds of frightful faces. I remembered that my father had warned me about these districts – "They are called 'rookeries', John. They have every evil on earth in there. They are not for the likes of us, my boy."

"Where are they?" I'd asked him.

"There is the rookery at the back of the Ratcliffe Highway. That's where they'll slit your throat to steal the buttons of your coat. Then there's Jacob's Island – the Venice of drains – in Bermondsey. You might come out alive, but who knows what disease you'll bring with you. And, of course, there's the Holy Land – at the end of New Oxford Street. That's where all the criminals gather. Even Mr Peel's policemen are frightened to go in there!" he laughed.

He would not have been laughing if he'd known that's where his son was now. The gang of boys was coming closer. I turned quickly and caught one with his hand on my school bag. He grinned and winked at me in a friendly way. "All right, guv?" he called.

The girl stopped on a corner by a noisy public house and spoke quickly to a man in a tall and battered hat. He nodded and began to walk towards me. When he was an arms-length away I stopped. I waited for him to attack me, but he stepped past me and grabbed one of the street urchins by the collar and said something quiet but fierce in his ear. He threw the boy to the ground. The boy wiped slime from his coat and scrambled away. The rest of the gang tumbled after him. The man touched the brim of his hat and showed me a black-toothed smile. "Pickpockets, sir," he said. "Have to watch out for them!"

"Th-thanks!" I stammered then hurried to the corner in time to see the girl standing at the doorway of a tall, narrow house between a theatre and a poor sort of hotel. The man who had rescued me leaned on the corner by the public house and watched me. I didn't think I'd be safe to go back. Ahead of me a large group of men blocked the road with some snarling dogs and I didn't feel I wanted to go forward. I stepped into the gloom of the house that the girl had entered.

There was no light here but a little late daylight through the doorway showed me a bare wooden stairway leading upwards. I caught the glimpse of a dark skirt whisking around the first landing and followed. When I reached the landing I saw she had climbed again. I followed. Each landing had five or six doors leading off it. Every one was closed.

On the fourth floor I heard a door opening. When I reached it I saw one door open. Candlelight spilled on to the wooden floor as I tiptoed over the creaking boards. I pushed the door gently and looked through the gap. The red-haired girl sat at a dressing table in front of a mirror. She wiped her eyes with a large silk handkerchief and I could see from her reflection that she had wiped away the grey circles underneath them. She looked more healthy now, her green eyes sparkling in the light of the candle.

Then she tugged at her ringlets and pulled them off. Her hair was quite short and she shook it till it fell into a neat frame around her thin face. Then she did something that made my heart stop. She looked into the reflection in the mirror and met my gaze. She grinned and said, "You caught me then?"

I cleared my throat, stepped into the room and tried to put on my best imitation of Mr Allison at his sternest. "Yes. I've caught *you*."

She turned slowly on the seat and peered at me mischievously. "Are you quite sure *you've* caught *me*?"

"What?" I said stupidly.

"Well, I mean, you're here in my room. You can't get out. Are you sure that I haven't caught you?" she asked.

"What do you mean, I can't get out?" I asked and my voice was beginning to rise in a squeak quite unlike Mr Allison.

"I mean that even if you got out of the door then my mates in the street wouldn't let you out of the Holy Land –

leastways, not with that fine shirt on your back and
money in your pocket!" she said.

My head was spinning now and I wondered how
the fearless hunter John de Vere had suddenly become
the frightened rabbit. "What do you mean, *if I* get out
of the door?"

"I mean," she said patiently, "if my dad will *let* you out!
Will you let him out, Dad?"

I felt the door swing shut behind me. The man had
been standing behind it. I looked at the tall man with
ginger whiskers and the fine but worn clothes. It was the
doctor who had arranged a collection of money for the girl.

"I might let him out, Ellie," the girl's father said.
"When we find out just what he wants."

3

They treated me well – for a prisoner. Ellie's father called himself 'Doctor' Morgan though he was actually a fishmonger by trade. "Red herring, jellied eels, pickled salmon," he told me. Now he was performing the doctor act because it helped Ellie with her begging and they scraped a living from that.

"But why don't you sell fish?" I asked.

Ellie Morgan laughed bitterly. "John, you live in another world. You may not have noticed but there's been a terrible slump in trade for the past five years. People are starving because they can't afford to buy our fish. We're starving because we can't sell it – at any price."

Mr Morgan explained more patiently, "Shopkeepers sell to people with money. But I'm a *coster*. I buy the cheapest fish I can and sell it off a barrow to the poorest people in the Holy Land. When the poorest people couldn't afford my fish we struggled to make a living. And the shopkeepers hate the costers. They get the police to move us on. One day a wheel broke on my barrow so I wasn't able to move. The police took the cart off me. It was everything I owned. I was finished." He shrugged. "Some day, if trade picks up, I may go back to selling fish."

"What you telling him all this for, dad?" Ellie cut in. "We want to know why he was following me. Probably one of them slave traders trying to kidnap me and sell me!" she said.

"No!" I cried. "I saw a man trying to kill the queen! I thought you saw him too and called after him. I wanted to know who he was!"

The girl flicked a glance at her father then narrowed her eyes. "And what if I do?" she said.

"Well . . ." I began. It was a good question. I hadn't thought this far ahead. I said weakly, "I thought we could go to the police."

She sat back on her stool and sneered. "Are you stupid?" she said.

"No."

"The less we have to do with the police the better. They'd want to know what dad and me were doing there for a start. We may be beggars but we've never been to prison, have we, dad?"

Mr Morgan shook his head. "Never."

"Anyway, I wouldn't want to see a poor man hang for pointing a pistol at a posh woman."

I found the courage to say, "What if he tries again and *kills* that posh woman?"

Ellie looked at her father.

"We'll have a word with him. Make sure he doesn't," Mr Morgan said quietly. "It's just all this Chartist excitement has gone to the poor boy's head," he said.

Father had told me about the Chartists. "Trouble-makers," he'd said. "They seem to think that every blessed man – from tramps and beggars to thieves and rogues – should be allowed to vote in parliamentary elections."

"*You* vote, father," I said.

"I am a respectable and responsible citizen and I have a house to prove it," he said. "One day you will have a vote, John. But you will be an educated and respected man by then. We cannot allow the country to be run by the common mob! We cannot be ruled by . . . the Dangerous Classes!" My father would have had one of his eye-bulging, teeth-baring, fist-clenching fits if he'd known I was in one of the dens of the Dangerous Classes.

I looked at the girl. "My father told me about the Chartist riots. I didn't know they planned to kill the queen."

"They don't!" she said impatiently. "The Chartists are a peaceful movement."

"*Some* of them," her father muttered.

"*Most* of them," Ellie said firmly. "The man who shot at the queen is a freak – he comes to the Chartist meetings, but he doesn't *listen*."

I thought about this for a moment. "But . . . if he tries again . . . and if he succeeds . . . then the Chartists will get the blame."

The room was silent apart from the soft sputtering of the candle. "The lad's right," Mr Morgan said finally. "We have to hand the man over to the police before he does something we'll all regret."

Ellie scowled but nodded slowly. "I suppose so. He's bound to be at the big meeting tonight," she said.

"*You're* Chartists?" I asked her. At that moment that seemed a worse crime than being street beggars and cheats.

"Of course!" she said. "It's the only hope we've got. Give us the vote and we'll change the government – change the government and they'll make life better for the rest of us. There's just been a huge Chartist rally in London. Mr Feargus O'Connor himself is coming to meet the people and speak tonight. Are you coming with us?"

"I should be getting home," I said weakly. "Father and mother will be worried."

Ellie threw back her head and snorted. "You wouldn't get past the street corner," she said. "Look, you have your school bag there. Have you got a pen and ink and paper?"

"Yes."

"Then write a message. I'll send Bill Bean to deliver it." She strode to the door and called down the dark stairwell, "Bill-ee-ee!" She returned and said, "You can trust Bill. He looks a little strange but that's because he used to be a chummie."

"A what?" I asked.

"A chummie. A chimney sweep," she explained. "It twisted his body but his mind's all right."

There was a soft knock on the door and Bill Bean shuffled in. He was no taller than a boy of nine though he must have been sixteen years old. His bowed legs and bent back made him still smaller. His face and hands were stained with years of soot. He looked up at me shyly as Ellie said, "Bill, this is young Master John. Will you take a message for him?"

"Yes, Miss Ellie," the sweep-boy said in a thin voice.

"Show Master John your knees and elbows, Bill," Mr Morgan said. "Master John doesn't quite understand how we live here in the Holy Land."

The boy rolled up his sleeves and trouser legs to show me the joints. His elbows and knees had thick pads of hard skin that shone as if they'd been polished. I winced and forced myself to look. "How did they get like that, Bill?" I asked.

The boy gave a shrug of a twisted shoulder and a shy smile. "Master did it to me. He was good to me, master was. At first I didn't like the chimneys – he put me up there and pricked my feet with a knife till I climbed."

"And you let him?" I asked. This master sounded far worse than Mr Allison and his cane. I'd never complain about him again, I decided.

"I was only six years old at the time," he said. "Mother sold me to the sweep. She'd have had to give the money back if I hadn't done the work."

I nodded. "What about your knees and elbows, Bill?"

"The master went to the pork shop and got salt water. He scrubbed it into my knees beside a hot fire. Made them go hard so I wouldn't scrape them," he explained.

"Didn't it hurt?"

"It did . . . but sometimes he beat me if I moved away from the fire . . . sometimes he gave me a halfpenny. In a year or so they were this hard. He was good my master was. Fed me and let me sleep on soot sacks with the other boys," he said.

"What happened to the master?" I asked.

Billy frowned. "They locked him away. One of the sweeps died and the police came to arrest the master. He nearly killed a policeman – so they sent him to jail. Now I got nobody to look after me," he said simply.

There was a long silence in the room. Mr Morgan spoke quietly at last. "So you see, Master John de Vere. *This* is the sort of person the Chartists want to help. People like me can always look after themselves. Bill Bean and his sort need a little help."

I nodded. I didn't trust myself to speak. I wrote the note quickly to my father and asked him to give the messenger a half-crown. After I'd explained to Bill where I lived he slipped from the room and left me with Ellie and her father.

"So, are you coming to the meeting tonight?" Ellie asked. "Find out the truth about the Chartists."

"And see if we can persuade that man not to kill the queen?" I added.

"Of course," Mr Morgan agreed.

"Then I'll come," I said.

"I'll make us something to eat and then it'll be time to go," Ellie said.

4

Ellie left the room and came back two minutes later with three slices of pie on a cracked plate. I looked for a knife and fork to eat with. The girl and her father said nothing but picked up a slice each and began to push it into their mouths as quickly as they could. My mother would have fainted if she could have seen them.

"Manners maketh the man, John," is what she always said whenever I made a slight mistake at the dinner table. I always had to use the right fork or spoon for each type of food.

"Eat up!" Ellie urged me, spitting crumbs as she spoke with a full mouth. By now my mother would have needed a bucketful of smelling salts to revive her from such a horror. I picked up the pie and began to nibble at it. The pastry tasted of stale flour and there was a mush of tasteless vegetables inside. I couldn't swallow it. I chewed and chewed and forced myself to let it slide down my throat.

I was starving but I said, "Sorry, I'm not very hungry."

The girl shrugged, took the rest of the pie from me, broke it in two and handed half to her father. He pushed the whole piece into his mouth happily then wiped his lips on his sleeve. "I like a piece of tapioca pie," he grinned.

Ellie held out her purse and rattled the money she had begged on Constitution Hill. "We can afford *meat* tomorrow, dad."

He smacked his lips noisily. "I like a bit of tapioca pie – but I like a steak pie better! Ever have steak pie, John?" he asked.

I nodded. I had soup, fish, meat, a pudding and cheese every evening for dinner. I simply ate what our cook made for us and never thought about it. "I sometimes have steak pie," I said.

I stopped. I realised that a large brown rat was snuffling at my feet for the crumbs I'd dropped. "Rat!" I gasped.

"Great!" Ellie whispered excitedly. "Catch it!"

"What!"

"Catch it. A good rat'll fetch sixpence at the pub," she said and began to move smoothly towards it.

"Sixpence? What for?" I squeaked.

"For rat fights, of course. Never been to a rat fight?"

I shook my head. My leg twitched and that made the rat scuttle away. Ellie groaned and shook her head. I could see she was disappointed in me. "Plenty more where that came from, I suppose," she said. "Shall we go then? See you later, dad?"

"I'll be there for the meeting," he nodded.

She led the way down the stairway. It was growing darker outside and I had to follow the sound of her feet on the stairs. There was a strong smell of vinegar and dead cats in the air. Together with the taste of that pie I was feeling sick. Even the filthy street seemed like fresh air after the house. Men and women seemed to be moving in the same direction as Ellie.

There wasn't a lot of light in those streets and I shuddered at the thought of what I was putting my shoes into. Ellie linked her arm through mine. "Stick close to me and you'll be safe," she said.

"Safe?" I almost squeaked.

"Yeah, you know? Nobody'll pick your pocket or drag you down an alley to steal your shirt."

"Would they do that?" I asked.

"'Course!" she laughed. "Get sixpence for a shirt like yours at a rag shop. That'll buy a couple of bottles of gin, won't it?"

"Will it? I don't drink gin."

"It's safer than drinking the water round here," she smiled. I could believe that. "The kids could sell your boots to Taff Hughes the fence for a shilling," she went on.

"They cost ten times as much!" I argued stupidly.

"They don't care. A shilling's a shilling and a shilling's a lot of money," she sniffed. "Four bottles of gin to be exact. Here, do you want a bottle of gin to take to the theatre now?" she asked.

"No," I said quickly. "I'm not thirsty."

She shrugged and muttered, "Funny boy."

As we rounded a corner we saw crowds of people pushing, elbowing and shouting as they forced their way into a doorway. Flares burned over the doorway and cast orange shadows over the sweating crowd. Ellie held me back. "This is the best place for a pickpocket to steal that sixpence in your jacket pocket," she whispered.

"How did you know . . ."

"I already looked," she grinned. "Don't worry. I put it back!"

An organ-grinder churned out a tune on his musical box while a wide-eyed monkey chattered and danced on his shoulder. I reached for my sixpence. Ellie noticed the movement of my hand. "Don't give him that!" she hissed. "It's the feller that gets to spend it on beer, not on the monkey, you know?"

I nodded. At last the crowd thinned and we made our way inside. Gas jets glowed brilliant white and made the packed hall hot. Sellers of pigs' trotters, ham sandwiches

and ale struggled to make their way through the crowds and struggled to make themselves heard through the din of laughter, shouting and babies bawling.

An orchestra was tuning up at the front near the stage. "I thought this was a Chartist meeting?" I cried to Ellie over the noise.

"It is. But people wouldn't come if there wasn't a bit of entertainment!" she called back, her lips close to my ear.

And when the orchestra struck up a tune and the curtains parted they settled for nearly an hour's entertainment. Singers who sang popular songs for the audience to join in, jugglers and acrobats and even a sailor who danced a hornpipe – while standing on his head!

At last a man in evening dress announced, "And now, ladies and gentlemen, we have the honour of presenting to you the editor of the *Northern Star* newspaper. The greatest man in the whole of the Chartist movement. Mr Feargus O'Connor himself!"

The crowd clapped – but not as enthusiastically as they had for the hornpipe dancer. Mr O'Connor stepped on to the stage and gave a short bow. "My friends . . ." he began and this raised a huge cheer. He was a handsome man, well-dressed and well-spoken with a slight Irish accent. The crowd was proud to be called his "friends".

"I do not need to tell you what the Chartist movement stands for. We stand for one vote for every man!" There was another huge cheer, but as it died down Ellie cried, "And what about the women?"

Mr O'Connor looked towards the girl . . . and so did two hundred pairs of eyes. "We must proceed one step at a time, my dear young lady. Votes for every man first . . . then votes for women later."

There was some grumbling among the men at this as if it wasn't such a popular idea. The speaker went on, "As you also know I took a petition to Parliament six weeks ago. That petition had three million, three hundred and seventeen thousand, seven hundred and fifty-two signatures on it. Our meeting on Kennington Common scared the authorities so much they sent Victoria to the Isle of Wight for safety!" There was jeering laughter and mutters of "Cowardly queen". O'Connor leaned forward and went on dramatically, "I can now tell you that Parliament has thrown out our petition by 222 votes to 17!"

There were groans this time from the crowd. As they died down, another voice called out. "So what are you going to do about it, Mr O'Connor?"

The voice came from the back of the hall. I turned to look at the man who had shouted. I froze. It was a young man and he wore a faded and ragged brown jacket. His wild eyes were burning with a fearsome anger . . . just as they had been when he pointed a gun at the queen!

5

I watched the man in the brown coat with my jaw dropped to my chest. "John Francis," Ellie murmured in my ear. I nodded and managed to close my mouth.

Feargus O'Connor was replying from the stage. His eyes were now shining in the gaslight as brightly as John Francis'. For a moment I thought I was watching two madmen talking and the rest of the audience didn't matter to them. "You know the motto of the Chartists, sir," O'Connor was saying. "Peaceful change if we can – forceful if we must."

"So when do we start to use force?" Francis called back. One or two in the audience were with him and muttered agreement.

"When peaceful means have failed," O'Connor said.

"When is that?"

"We will know when the time comes," O'Connor said fiercely.

"And what will you *do*?" Francis said in a jeering voice. "Go on strike? The workers will starve while the factory owners and the land owners live on their fat." There were still more cheers for this. Francis was encouraged and went on, "In the Midlands they've been trying to wreck industry by knocking plugs out of boilers. Is that the best you have to offer? We didn't join the Chartists to knock plugs out of boilers. That's work for children!"

On the stage O'Connor was becoming angry. "And what would you do, my good sir?"

"Kill the queen! She's not in the Isle of Wight now. She's parading around the streets of London in her fancy carriage with her German joke of a husband. I saw them! Laughing! Laughing because she thinks we are beaten! Kill her!" Francis cried.

In all that crowd there was a sudden and a dreadful silence. No one could quite believe he had said it. O'Connor relaxed a little and gave a grim smile. "Did you not know, sir, you *cannot* kill a queen. The moment Victoria dies then her baby son becomes king."

"Then kill him too!" Francis roared, his face red and angry, eyes bulging.

"Then the next in line takes over the throne! Don't you understand? Our only hope is to take control of the country through Parliament . . . and the people will only control Parliament when every man has the vote!"

Half the audience seemed to be on O'Connor's side. Each remark brought cheers from one side or jeers from the other. The meeting was slipping out of control. Francis at last managed to make his voice heard. "So what sort of action are you going to take now this petition has failed?" Dozens of voices joined in repeating the question.

O'Connor held up a hand for silence. "I am not prepared to say."

"Coward!" a little man with a beard shouted at him.

O'Connor looked down angrily. "No, my friend. I am no *coward*. I am merely *careful*. We must not betray our plans to the government. Do you not realise that they have their spies everywhere? In this very audience there are members of Mr Peel's police force! He has formed a new group of detectives who wear plain clothes, not uniforms!"

Several things began to happen at that point. Most of

the audience started to cry out angrily at the thought of spies in their midst and quite a few began accusing strangers in the audience. Fights broke out and fists began to fly. I caught a glimpse of John Francis. His face had turned pale and shocked at the thought of police spies. He pushed past a group of women with babies that had begun to squall and disappeared through the darkened doorway. Half a second later the man beside me forced his way towards the same door.

The tall, hard-faced man was dressed in old, worn clothes yet they didn't smell as badly as some of the others I'd stood among. I knew at once he was one of the police spies that O'Connor had said was in the audience. I also knew that I had to tell him everything that had happened on Constitution Hill that afternoon.

"Where you going?" Ellie asked, grabbing the tail of my coat and letting me pull her through the audience.

"To tell that policeman everything," I hissed.

"Not without me, mate," she said and clung tighter.

We hurried down the stairs that were dimly lit after the gas-lit glare of the theatre. The hard-faced man stood at the bottom and peered into the still darker street. Ellie called, "You'll not catch him, officer. He knows every rat-run and coal hole in this rookery."

The man glared at her, looked at me then back at the girl. "Tell me where to find him or I'll arrest you," he growled.

"Haven't a clue," she said lightly and cheekily. I knew that he was about to arrest her there and then.

"Excuse me, sir," I said politely as I knew. "I think I may be able to help you."

He squinted at me and said, "You don't look or sound as if you belong here."

"I don't, sir. You see, I saw that man point a gun at Queen Victoria this afternoon. I followed him here," I explained.

"Come with me," the man said.

"Don't go, John," Ellie said. "He's probably trying to kidnap you and sell you into slavery."

The man sighed. "I am Police Officer Restiaux and you can come with me now or I will call for police assistance and have you carried away."

"Where you taking him?" Ellie asked. "He goes nowhere without me."

"Are you his guardian angel?" Restiaux asked.

"More like a guardian devil," she replied and pulled back her lips in a false and defiant grin.

The officer sighed. "Very well, you can come too. But you'll have to button your insolent lip, young madam."

"Ooooh! Why, Mister Policeman. Where we going? Buckingham Palace?"

"Exactly," the man said quietly. "Buckingham Palace."

6

The thought of a visit to Victoria's home quietened even Ellie's babbling tongue. Officer Restiaux led the way through the dank streets that were filled with snuffling vermin and muffled moanings and cryings from miserable humans. I felt the eyes watching us and heard the laughter in the gin palaces go quiet as we passed them. We seemed to walk these hostile streets surrounded by hatred but untouched by it.

At last we arrived in New Oxford Street where the lights and the clatter of traffic was a welcome relief. Restiaux signalled for a hansom cab. We climbed aboard and at last he relaxed a little and began to talk. I explained exactly what I'd seen – despite Ellie trying to help and confusing him.

It was a slow journey through the streets that were now filled with crowds going to the theatre – more respectable theatres than the one we'd just left. As we drove down Constitution Hill the officer stopped the cab and I had to show him just where John Francis had stood when he raised the pistol. He shook his head and said, "Amazing!"

"You don't believe me?" I asked.

"Oh, I *believe* you," he said seriously. "I meant that it's amazing that this Francis fired from *that* spot. You may remember that a man called Edward Oxford fired two shots at the queen back in 1840. He fired from exactly the same place."

"You think John Francis was copying Edward Oxford?" Ellie asked.

"It's possible. Oxford was a feeble-minded youth – only about eighteen – but his room was stuffed full of leaflets about revolution."

"But he wasn't a Chartist!" Ellie argued.

"No-o," Restiaux admitted. "Not exactly . . ."

"And John Francis isn't *exactly* a Chartist either," she went on. "So don't go trying to blame the Chartists for shooting at the queen!"

"No one is blaming anyone yet. We have to catch this Francis first and then decide why he did it later," the officer said calmly.

"What happened to Oxford?" I asked, trying to calm the argument between the policeman and the girl.

Restiaux stroked his long, smooth chin and said, "He was sentenced to death for treason," he replied. "They later decided that he was insane and let him live. They locked him in a lunatic asylum. He's still there now. The queen was furious."

"Because he shot at her?" I asked.

"No. Because they let Oxford live. She said that anyone shooting at the queen should be executed so that others would see what happened to assassins. She thought that letting Oxford live would encourage others to take shots at her."

"And it looks like she was right," I sighed.

We climbed back into the cab and trotted on till we reached the palace. When we went to a side entrance another shock awaited us. A man met us and showed us into an office. Officer Restiaux pulled his hat off and stood to attention.

"Who's he?" Ellie whispered.

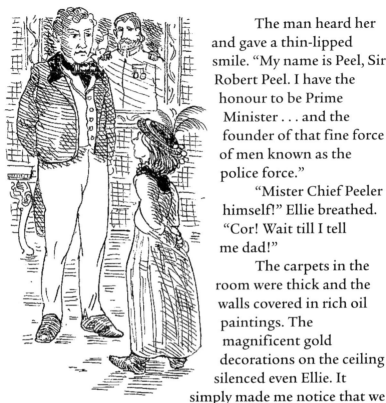

The man heard her and gave a thin-lipped smile. "My name is Peel, Sir Robert Peel. I have the honour to be Prime Minister . . . and the founder of that fine force of men known as the police force."

"Mister Chief Peeler himself!" Ellie breathed. "Cor! Wait till I tell me dad!"

The carpets in the room were thick and the walls covered in rich oil paintings. The magnificent gold decorations on the ceiling silenced even Ellie. It simply made me notice that we were carrying the stench of the Holy Land in our clothes. I repeated my story to Sir Robert Peel while he listened very seriously. Finally he rose and said, "I want you to repeat the story once more."

"Now?" I asked.

"No. I want the prince to hear it."

"Prince," I echoed stupidly.

"The queen's husband. Prince Albert. He called me here tonight. He will take a particular interest in this. You'll see why," Peel explained. "Bow when you meet him and call him sir. Can you curtsey, girl?"

Ellie shrugged. "I can try . . . but I might fall over."

Peel scowled at her then turned and walked through doors that were about large enough to let Albert enter in his carriage. In fact he walked in. I bowed low while Ellie gave a bob and a giggle.

The prince sat behind a desk while I had to stand facing him. He was a thin, pale young man with a fine moustache and dark eyes. He spoke with a thick German accent. "Thank you for coming, young man and young lady," he smiled. "I understand you witnessed an interesting incident this afternoon."

"Yes, sir," Ellie and I said together. Albert steepled his fingers and listened carefully while we repeated it for the third time.

"That is good," he said. "I too saw the man with the gun, you see? The queen saw nothing. The *soldiers* who were riding on guard saw nothing and the *driver* saw nothing. When I told Sir Robert Peel what had happened I think he thought I was losing my mind!"

Peel spluttered and tried to say that he thought no such thing but the prince waved away his objections with a flap of his hand. "I am so pleased that I am not mad," he said lightly. "You British people would then have an excuse to get rid of me!"

Peel had turned practically purple with shock by now but Prince Albert went on. "Tell me, girl, do you know this John Francis, the man with the gun?"

"Yes, majesty."

"What sort of man is he?"

Ellie creased her face. "I don't know him very well, you understand. He's a funny sort of feller. Keeps himself to himself. He's a cabinetmaker."

"And a Chartist?" the Prince asked.

"Never seen him at a meeting before," Ellie said and I knew that was a lie. "But then there were lots of strangers there tonight to see the great Mr O'Connor himself."

The prince nodded. "Officer Restiaux, you saw this man, John Francis?"

"Yes, sir."

"And, in your opinion, is he a danger to the queen?"

Restiaux cleared his throat. "Until he is arrested he is a great danger."

"And how do you propose to catch him?"

"Search for him in the area where he was last seen . . ."

"Won't work!" Ellie cut in to the annoyance of the men in the room. "Sorry, but I already explained. He can disappear like a rat down a sewer. There's a secret entrance to the Holy Land that you'll never find. It's a tunnel through a timber yard to the east. Criminals get in and out even when the police watch all the other entries to this rookery. You'll never get him if you go after him."

"So?" the prince asked. "How do you catch a rat?"

"You put bait down don't you. Tempt him to come out into the open," the girl told him.

"And the bait that will bring Mr Francis into the open . . . is the queen riding out in her carriage," Prince Albert said. "Precisely my thoughts."

"But the risk!" Sir Robert exploded.

"The risk is for the queen to take."

"As the prime minister I insist . . ." Peel began.

"And as prince consort I insist," the German said. "You will, of course, make sure that your men are there in force, in plain clothes, when we ride out tomorrow."

"You're setting her majesty up as a decoy duck! What if something goes wrong?" Peel objected weakly.

"Then the blame will be all mine, Sir Robert," the prince told him. He rose to his feet, nodded briefly at Ellie and me then strode out of the room.

The prime minister looked angry and worried.

"Cor! Fancy using the queen as a bit of bait," Ellie said. "I hope John Francis is a rotten shot."

"So do I," Sir Robert said. "So do I."

7

Officer Restiaux took me home in a hansom cab, saying he'd need to talk to my father about security and the need for secrecy. When we arrived in the driveway a small figure slipped from the shadows at the side of the house. "It's Bill Bean!" Ellie said. "Evening, Bill! What you still doing here?"

The sweep came shyly up to the cab as we stepped down. "The gentleman took the message," he explained. "Then he sent me down to the kitchen to get some supper."

I sometimes think my father has a kind heart, though he tries hard to hide it.

"What you get?" Ellie asked eagerly.

"Meat, Miss Ellie. Lots of meat. More than I see in a month . . . or even a year!" the boy sighed.

"Take Ellie back to the kitchen door, Bill," I said. "Cook will give *her* some too."

"May God bless you, is the prayer of your unhappy but true friend!" Ellie whined in her beggar's voice, then grinned to show me it was her little joke.

Officer Restiaux led me to the front door and I faced a further hour of questions from father before I was finally allowed to go to bed. Father was in his most serious mood. Mother was more concerned by the smell I'd brought into the house on my clothes. At last I was allowed to leave the library.

I hurried to the kitchens and found Ellie chatting happily to Cook while Bill Bean sat quietly in a corner. "I came to say goodbye, Ellie. And to thank you for taking care of me in the Holy Land."

"Any time," she smiled. "It was worth it to get the sort of scran your cook's just given me! In fact it even made me feel a bit guilty," she admitted.

"For what?" I asked.

She took a deep breath. "For stealing that sixpence out of your pocket," she said and pushed the coin into my hand.

I didn't know quite what to do. Stupidly I said, "Thank you. Thank you . . . and goodbye."

"Goodbye!" she blinked. "You're going to see me again, aren't you?"

"Well, I . . ."

"I *mean* you're going to be there tomorrow afternoon for the shooting party, aren't you?" she urged.

I hadn't thought about it. "I suppose so," I said.

"Right you are then! See you there. Come on, Billy," she said. First she turned to go then she swung back suddenly, placed her hands on my shoulders, and kissed me on the cheek. I turned redder than her hair and cook almost exploded as she tried to keep her laughter in.

* * *

The next day at school was one of my worst. I thought of nothing but John Francis shooting the queen. How could Prince Albert allow her to take the risk? My mind was not on my work and Mr Allison made me pay for my wandering mind with endless thrashings. I was not allowed to say a word about the adventures of the day before or the one that was due to happen that afternoon.

I stumbled wearily out of school into the May sunshine and finally reached Constitution Hill. There were a few more people here today. The extra numbers were men; burly men looking around constantly. Ellie came up to me. She was wearing her ringlets and grey shadows round the eyes. "You're begging today?" I asked.

"Why not? Lurkers don't get holidays, you know!"

"No . . . I suppose not . . . but with so many policemen around . . . ."

"Nah! They've got more to worry about than a starving orphan like me," she groaned pitifully.

"You're not an orphan. Your father's still alive."

She blinked and looked at me with an annoyed frown. "*They* don't know that, you glock!"

I didn't know what a glock was but it didn't sound like a compliment. "Is John Francis here yet?" I asked.

"No, but Bill Bean is!" she smiled. The sweep boy looked more sickly and pathetic in the daylight than he had in the dinginess of the Holy Land. His wide eyes roamed through the crowd. "John's going to shoot the queen," he said.

"It's supposed to be a secret!" I squeaked.

"Bill Bean won't tell," Ellie told me. I shrugged.

"John Francis is going to be famous," Bill Bean said. "A hero of the working classes."

"Where did you learn words like that, Bill?"

Bill looked down at his feet. His boots had been too small for him so the toes were cut out. "Meetings," he mumbled.

"Bill," I said. "Why not use that half-crown my father gave you to buy a new pair of boots?"

"Spent it," he said in a whisper and refused to look up.

"On what?"

Before he could reply I sensed a stir in the crowd. I craned my neck to look up the hill and saw the queen's carriage appear at the top. The horses were trotting quickly. The policemen who had been facing the road turned round and stared into the crowd.

No one, not even John Francis, would try to shoot the queen from the same spot on a second day, I decided. The carriage drew closer. I could hear the patter of applause from the spectators as it passed them.

I saw the queen with a tense, half-frozen smile on her face. She was afraid. Albert sat beside her. He waved a hand at no one in particular while his eyes darted among the watching people. I caught his eye, and his wave, just for an

instant, was directed at me.

"Hello, Bertie!" Ellie cried.

Thank goodness he wouldn't hear her over the clatter of hooves and the rattle of carriage wheels. But over that rushing sound I heard another. The wordless cry of a man. The frightened scream of a woman. I turned in time to see John Francis burst through the crowd and rush to the side of the carriage.

He raised his arm and everyone could see he held a pistol. He was just five paces from the queen. Policemen barged and stumbled after him but I knew they were too late. Francis had a clear shot. His arm followed the movement of the carriage. His finger tightened on the trigger.

As the startled queen drew level he squeezed the trigger. At the same moment Officer Restiaux reached him and swung his officer's stick at that arm. The gun clicked but there was no explosion.

The coachman whipped the horses into a gallop while the other policemen leapt on to John Francis and dragged him, struggling, away from the road.

"He could never hope to get away with it," I said, shaking my head. Ellie looked at me. She didn't need make-up to look pale. She looked as shocked as I felt. "But he almost did. He *nearly* got away with it," she gasped.

"Why did he do it?" I asked.

"Because he's a hero," Bill Bean said. His eyes were sparkling in his thin, pitiful face. "Because we hate her."

"We, Billy? Who hates the queen? The Chartists?"

But he wriggled away from my hand on his shoulder and disappeared into the crowd. John Francis was under arrest. Were there any other killers lurking out there in the gutters of London or the slums of Britain? And when might the next one strike?

I didn't know how close I was to the answer.

Part Two

The Fact Files

1. THE PEOPLE FILE

No one had ever assassinated a monarch of England before. What sort of people would try in 1842 . . . and why?

Feargus O'Connor

Name: *Feargus O'Connor*

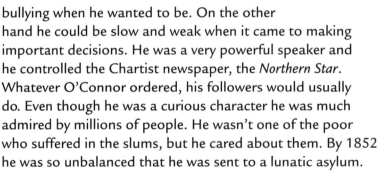

Appearance: Good-looking and well-spoken, with an Irish accent.

Character: Very temperamental. He wanted to be the one and only leader of the Chartists. O'Connor was boastful and bullying when he wanted to be. On the other hand he could be slow and weak when it came to making important decisions. He was a very powerful speaker and he controlled the Chartist newspaper, the *Northern Star*. Whatever O'Connor ordered, his followers would usually do. Even though he was a curious character he was much admired by millions of people. He wasn't one of the poor who suffered in the slums, but he cared about them. By 1852 he was so unbalanced that he was sent to a lunatic asylum.

Problem: Other Chartists believed they could quietly persuade the government to change – Feargus O'Connor believed that they could threaten and bully the government with force and violence. How far would he go with these threats of violence to get what he wanted? And how far would his supporters go? O'Connor could never say to his followers, "Kill the queen!" in public. That would be treason and he could have been executed for it. But was he mad enough to *encourage* someone secretly?

Police today say you need to understand the 'victim' if you want to understand the criminal. Victoria died in 1901 as a well-loved, popular old lady. Why would anyone want to murder her?

Queen Victoria

Name: *Queen Victoria*

Appearance: Very short; a plump, round face with thin, unsmiling lips

Character: Very cold and regal. She was very distant to the ordinary people of Britain and not at all popular when she first came to the throne in 1837. Victoria's husband, her German cousin Albert, was even less popular. Of course the upper classes supported her at first until one of Victoria's ladies-in-waiting was dying and the queen cruelly dismissed her! This turned even the upper classes against her. When Edward Oxford tried to shoot Victoria in 1840 she became a little more popular again. She was quite determined that anyone who tried to kill her should be executed. It was only in her last years, the 1880s and 1890s, that the people took Victoria to their hearts – most people had known no other monarch. But, at first, she was not much loved.

Problem: Who would want to kill Victoria in 1842? She was unpopular but, if she died, then the baby Edward would become 'king, though everyone knew the real ruler would be his father, the unpopular Prince Albert. Some Chartists swore they would get votes for everyone even if they had to spill the blood of the upper classes – but no Chartist ever seems to have suggested killing the queen. And, if the Chartists did kill her, would it make them more or less popular? Of course, throughout history, there have always been individuals who have assassinated leaders for no very good reason.

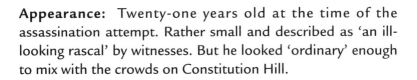

Historians have written thousands of words about Feargus O'Connor and millions about Queen Victoria, but most pay very little attention to 'ordinary' people like John Francis.

John Francis

Name: *John Francis*

Appearance: Twenty-one years old at the time of the assassination attempt. Rather small and described as 'an ill-looking rascal' by witnesses. But he looked 'ordinary' enough to mix with the crowds on Constitution Hill.

Character: He had a respectable job as a cabinetmaker and he was not from one of the desperately poor families in the slums of London. His father also had a reasonable job in the theatre at Covent Garden. When he was sent for trial the judges decided he was not insane – he knew what he was doing when he twice aimed a pistol at the queen. When he lost his nerve after the first attempt, he walked away muttering, "Fool that I was not to fire." Would he draw attention to himself like this? He had to be fairly intelligent to plan the attempts and angry enough to carry them through.

Problem: Was John Francis acting on his own? Did he simply decide one day that he would kill the queen? (It was easy enough to buy a weapon – though loading it and using it needed some training and skill.) Or was John Francis put up to this job by other people? If so, who were they? Chartists? There were other groups trying to change the way the government ran the country. Some wanted changes in the way food prices were fixed (by the Corn Laws) and some in the way the poor were treated in poorhouses (by the Poor Law). They were all very active in 1842. Was John Francis carried away by all the excitement and talk of revolution?

2. THE TIME FILE

1793   Over in France the poor peasants finally decide they have suffered too much misery under their kings. They begin a revolution and send the king and queen to the guillotine. This is followed by a reign of terror in which many of the upper classes are executed. In Britain the government are terrified that the poor in Britain will try to copy the example of the French so in . . .

1799   when Napoleon Bonaparte takes control of France, Britain joins other countries to fight his armies. They plan to put kings back on the throne of France. By . . .

1805   Napoleon's armies have conquered large areas of Europe. Britain's navy defeat the French at the Battle of Trafalgar and this leaves Britain and Russia as the only countries in Europe free from Napoleon's rule. The struggle goes on until . . .

1815   Napoleon is finally defeated at the Battle of Waterloo (in Belgium). Louis XVIII becomes king of France. The British army leader, the Duke of Wellington, returns home a national hero. His thousands of soldiers return home to find no work, high food prices (fixed by the Corn Laws) and hunger. Their homes are filthy slums and the 'winners' of the Napoleonic wars think they deserve better lives. They begin to demand a vote for every man so they can put things right in government. The French Revolution may be over but the danger of an English revolution is growing. In . . .

1819   a meeting of 50,000 people in St Peter's Fields, Manchester, demands the vote. Eleven are killed and 400 injured when the army attacks them. The working classes can't seem to win through violence. Discontent continues.

1837   Queen Victoria comes to the throne. The Chartist organisation is formed. Chartists want to organise petitions for peaceful change and votes for every man. In . . .

1839   a one-million signature petition has no effect and a rebellion in Wales simply leads to the deaths of fourteen Chartists and the organisation begins to die until . . .

1840   Irishman Feargus O'Connor takes over leadership of the Chartists. He brings more violent and revolutionary ideas to the Chartists. Edward Oxford tries to shoot Queen Victoria. Sir Robert Peel's new police force investigate and 'revolutionary' leaflets are found in Oxford's room. But he is proved to be insane and the only effect of his actions is to make Victoria more popular. Then . . .

1842   trade is bad, prices are high, people are starving and out of work. The Chartists are more popular than ever. Their new petition now has three million signatures and is six *miles* long! But again it does them no good. Then John Francis tries to assassinate Victoria – *twice*. The new London police capture him and the threat of revolution dies down again until . . .

1848   a second revolution in France gets rid of French kings for good. The Chartists, led by O'Connor, raise a six-million signature petition. Unfortunately many signatures are jokes and the petition fails. The Chartists never recover and in . . .

1852   they lose their leader when O'Connor goes mad and is locked away in an asylum. Trade and employment improve, and as people begin to earn a little more the threat of an English revolution fades. Victoria reigns over a more peaceful country despite occasional attacks on her by lone assassins and in . . .

1901   Victoria dies after reigning longer than any British monarch. She had survived fears of an English revolution . . . and eight attempts on her life.

3. THE LIFESTYLE FILE

What was life like for people in Victorian Britain? Was it so bad that they would want a revolution like the French?

Victorian children

It wasn't easy being the child of a poor family in Victorian times. Sickness and disease killed many at an early age. Only half lived to their fifth birthday!

And those who reached the grand old age of six or more found they were expected to work to help the family make a living. If you couldn't make a living then you ended up in the dreaded 'workhouse'. That's why they took on dreadful jobs like sweeping chimneys.

Sweeps

Boy sweeps usually began work about four in the morning, before fires were lit in houses. They worked for twelve hours. They'd have probably worked longer but by evening most houses had blazing fires.

The owner of a house should have let the fire go cold if they were expecting a sweep – many didn't bother so the sweeps climbed up the chimneys full of hot, choking fumes. A Manchester sweep describes the life . . .

When you're learning a child you can't be too soft with him; you must use violence. I shudder now when I think of it. I myself have gone to bed with my knee and elbow scraped and raw and the inside of my thighs all scratched. We slept five or six boys in a kind of cellar with soot bags over us, sticking to the wounds sometimes. That, and some straw, were all our bedclothes. Dozens of sweeps die of lung diseases and they are filthy in their habits. Lads often wear one shirt right on till it's done with. I have been fifteen months without being washed except by the rain. Why, I've almost been walking away with the lice on my body.

A second sweep said . . .

The usual age for boys to begin sweeping is from six upwards. I begin myself at a little over five. They are generally the children of the poorest and worst-behaved parents who want to get rid of them and make a little bit of money by it as well. It's as bad as the slave trade only not so well known. The women are harder than the men when it comes to using boy sweeps. A woman who had just sent her son to a sweep followed me in the street recently. She threatened to pull my hair because I'd spoken out against children sweeping. I myself used to use boys as young as five and a half years, but I don't like them. They can die as suddenly and quietly as you might fall asleep in that chair by the fire. I've known eight or nine sweeps lose their lives by sooty cancer. There is no cure for it once it has begun.

There was even a slave trade in boy sweeps. One master sweep reported . . .

Nottingham is famous for climbing boys. This is on account of the chimneys being so narrow in that town. A Nottingham boy is worth more to sell. A boy of about seven or eight was stolen from me once. As he was in the street a man seized him by the arms. He carried the boy off to a lodging house and stupefied him with drugged tea. After the tea the child fell into a deep sleep and lost all his appetite. An inspector and I traced him to Hull. The boy was ever so glad to see his 'master' had come for him. The thief said that if they had got him on a ship across to France they could have got £10 for him.

By the time a boy reached sixteen he was usually too large to get into chimneys and had to give up climbing. The trouble was he would be too weak and twisted in his body to do almost anything else. There was one job he could still do well – he could become a 'snakesman'.

A snakesman would climb into the narrowest of windows and enter a house. He would then unbar the door of the house and let his partners in to steal whatever they could. This is, of course, illegal but some sweep boys were naturally good at it after years of squeezing up chimneys. Some snakesmen weren't even *retired* sweep boys – they were still sweeping in the daytime and breaking into houses at night. The master sweep would often charge a hire fee for the boy to go off with a burglar.

A young man called Williams was a snakesman and a brilliant climber. He had once been sent up the inside of a twelve-metre factory chimney. When he got to the top he decided to run away from his master. He couldn't climb back down the inside – his master was waiting – so he climbed down the *outside* and escaped to freedom that way.

He turned to burglary but was eventually caught and in 1836 was sentenced to hang for his crimes. He then discovered his climbing skills had still another use – escaping from prison! Williams . . .

✗ climbed a fifteen-metre wall
✗ crawled along the top – even though it was protected by revolving spikes which cut him
✗ jumped down three metres on to a roof
✗ crossed the prison roof until he reached the roofs of nearby houses where he saw a woman hanging out washing
✗ jumped down into her yard and away down the streets
He was hidden by people who would not betray him. They believed that hanging someone for theft was too harsh.

Behave like a gentleman

John may have been shocked by Ellie's behaviour. But would he be shocked by yours? Try these problems to see if you could have been accepted by polite Victorians. Just one problem . . . if you make a single mistake you could well be frowned on for the rest of your life!

1. *Do/Don't* . . . bite straight into your bread.
2. *Do/Don't* . . . call your servants 'girls'
3. *Do/Don't* . . . raise your hat to a lady in the street.
4. *Do/Don't* . . . spit on the pavement.
5. *Do/Don't* . . . sit with your legs crossed.
6. *Do/Don't* . . . offer your hand to an older person to be shaken.
7. *Do/Don't* . . . drink from the side of your soup spoon and not the end.
8. *Do/Don't* . . . write to people you know on postcards.
9. *Do/Don't* . . . remove your overcoat before you enter someone's living room.
10. *Do/Don't* . . . use slang words.

Answers

1. *Don't* bite bread. Break off a piece and place it in your mouth.

2. *Don't* call servants 'girls'. Call them maids or servants.

3. *Do* raise your hat to a lady friend. *But* . . . wait till she has bowed to you first and do not wave your hat in the air the way the French do. Put it straight back on to your head. If she offers to shake hands then you may do so. If you are smoking then take your cigar out of your mouth with one hand as you raise your hat with the other.

4. *Don't* spit on the pavement – or anywhere else for that matter!

5. *Don't* sit with your legs crossed, it is *extremely* impolite.

6. *Don't* offer your hand to an older person. Wait until they have offered a hand to you.

7. *Do* drink from the side of your soup spoon – and remember you mustn't gurgle or suck in your breath while you sip your soup.

8. *Don't* use postcards. Write letters or nothing at all.

9. *Do* remove your overcoat when entering someone's living room – even if you are only making a very short call.

10. *Don't* use slang words . . . usually. There are some slang words that a gentleman may use. If you don't know what they are then avoid slang altogether.

Behave like a lady

Trying to be a lady was probably harder than trying to be a gentleman. Can you get the rules right?

1. You are given a jelly to eat. To eat it do you use
   a) your knife
   b) your fork
   c) your spoon

2. You are given cheese and bread. You cut a small piece of cheese with your knife then . . .
   a) pop it into your mouth with the knife
   b) put it on to a piece of bread and use your fingers
      to put the bread and cheese into your mouth
   c) put the cheese on to a plate and use
your fingers to put it in your mouth.

3. You need garters to hold up your
stockings. Do you wear them . . .
   a) below the knee
   b) on the knee
   c) above the knee

4. A gentleman asks you to dance.
Do you reply . . .
   a) push off
   b) I will give you a dance if you come
back a little later. I have promised
the next three to other gentlemen
   c) I shall be delighted to

5. A lady offers you her hand. Do you . . .
   a) press it gently
   b) shake it
   c) refuse to take it

6. When you visit another lady you must
take a 'visiting card'. Hand this to the servant who answers
the door so the owner of the house knows who is calling.

This visiting card must be:
  a) the same size as a gentleman's
  b) smaller than a gentleman's card
  c) larger than a gentleman's card
7. A married lady sleeps . . .
  a) in a long-sleeved nightdress that reaches to the floor
  b) in a short-sleeved nightdress that reaches below the knees
  c) in pyjamas.
8. Make-up should . . .
  a) not be worn
  b) be in bright, lively colours to match your dress
  c) be so light no one can tell you are wearing any

Answers
1. b) Eat jelly, blancmanges and ices with a fork.
2. b) Make sure you don't touch the cheese with your fingers. Never eat off the end of your knife and young ladies never ever eat cheese at a dinner party any way.
3. c) It is quite disgraceful to wear a garter below the knee! Of course no one ever saw your legs – or even your ankles – so how would they know?
4. b) Don't reject a man – even if you hate the sight of him. On the other hand, don't seem too keen – even if you are!
5. a) And don't forget to smile!
6. a) When you leave you should also leave two of your husband's cards on the hall table. If you are unmarried and living with your mother then you shouldn't have your own card anyway.
7. a) Four-poster beds had curtains to keep draughts out. The Victorians began to use brass beds instead. Lots of draughts, so those long nightdresses would be useful on a winter night.
8. c) Popular Victorian actresses wore lipstick, cheek colour and eyeliners . . . but they were considered really rather 'common'.

Feeding the famished

The poor in the city slums didn't have time for good manners. A visiting writer called Henry Mayhew was horrified by the way people lived. By himself he could do little to help them, but he tried. One night he gave a feast for thirty beggars in a slum boarding-house . . . though fifty turned up when they heard about the treat. If Ellie's manners shocked John in the story then imagine what he'd have thought if he'd been at Henry Mayhew's feast . . .

The dinner was then portioned out into twenty-five platefuls, all the plates that the boarding house owned. It was handed out through a small window in the kitchen to each man as his name was called out. As he hurried to the seat behind the bare table, he commenced tearing the meat asunder with his fingers, for knives and forks were unknown here. Some, it is true, used bits of wood like skewers but this seemed almost too polite for words in a place like this. Others sat on the ground with the plate of meat and pudding on their legs. A beggar boy, immediately on receiving his portion, whirled the plate round on his thumb as he went. Then, dipping his nose in the plate, seized a potato in his mouth.

Do *not* try this trick in your own home or the school dining hall!

It is easy to see why there was such a gap between the rich and the poor. It was not just a matter of the money they had. The two groups behaved in completely different ways. A poor person (like Ellie) could hope to make money . . . but how could they ever learn how to behave?

Talk like a trasseno

Trassenos were villains. They had their own way of life in the slums of Victorian Britain . . . they also had their own language. What would you say to a trasseno if he (or she) said these things to you? Would you answer 'Yes' or 'No'? Be careful! Give the wrong answer and something very nasty might happen . . .

1. "Do you fancy a chat?" *Yes/No*
2. "Would you like me to nail your broken door?" *Yes/No*
3. "Shall I give you this finny?" *Yes/No*
4. "Do you think teachers should give their pupils dewskitches?" *Yes/No*
5. "How about a ride on my flummut horse?" *Yes/No*
6. "Are you flat?" *Yes/No*
7. "Would you like to put a jack under the wheel of my carriage?" *Yes/No*
8. "Is your father a nammo?" *Yes/No*
9. "Shall I invite some jolly people to your party?" *Yes/No*
10. "Do you wear a flag when you are cooking?" *Yes/No*

Answers:
1. A 'chat' is a louse that crawls around your body. Are you sure you fancy one?
2. To 'nail' something is to 'steal' it. And doors were popular for sleeping on. Prop one up on a few bricks and it keeps you out of the damp pools on the floor – unfortunately it's not high enough to keep the rats off you.

3. A 'finny' is a five pound note. But be careful . . . a trasseno might try to give you some flash money – worthless imitation money. The forgers didn't try to copy money – that was a serious offence and you could be hanged for it until 1832. Instead they made notes that looked like money, but with 'The Bank of Engraving' written on instead of 'The Bank of England'.

4. A 'dewskitch' is a beating – usually with a strap, a birch (a bundle of twigs) or a cane. Girls were not beaten as often as boys.

5. 'Flummut' means dangerous.

6. A 'flat' person isn't someone who's been run over by a flummut horse! It's a person who is easily tricked.

7. Probably not. A 'jack' was trasseno language for a policeman. Of course policemen were also called Peelers because they were organised by Sir Robert Peel. Bob is short for Robert so they were also called 'Bobbies'.

8. Probably not. 'Nammo' should really be spelled 'namow' because it means 'woman' (spelled backwards). Most of these slipped out of use – we no longer say 'yennep' for a 'penny' or 'tol' for 'lot'. No one drinks 'reeb' any more or calls a policeman an 'esclop'. But a few *are* still used – you may be a 'yob' yourself!

9. A 'jolly' person is one who starts a fight in public! They can be quite useful; they start a fight and when everyone is watching it the fine wirers, flimps and gonophs (pickpockets) can get to work stealing unguarded purses.

10. You should. 'Flag' means apron.

Mr Peel's poor police

Officer Restiaux in the story was one of the new police force created in 1829 by Sir Robert Peel. Restiaux was an expert on the Holy Land. He knew many of its secrets and many of its villains. Still, it was another matter trying to arrest them in the shelter of their rookery.

When Robert Peel formed the London police force in 1829 they were not at all popular. Many people, especially the poor, saw them as spies for the government.

In *The Pirates of Penzance*, a comic opera by Gilbert and Sullivan published in 1879, the policemen sing 'A policeman's lot is not a happy one.' But in the force's early years it was even worse! Look at these facts and decide if *you* would like to have been a policeman in Victoria's Britain . . .

1. In the early years of the police force crowds gathered in the streets and pelted 'Peel's bloody gang' with rotten fruit and vegetables. Children jeered at police with the rhyme: "I spy blue, I spy black! I spy a peeler in a shiny hat." This warned criminals that a policeman was in the area.

2. The first police uniforms were not comfortable. PC Cavanagh described how he was dressed on his first day: "When I looked at myself in the mirror I wondered why on earth I had decided to become a Peeler. My top hat was slipping all over my head, my boots were two sizes too large and were rubbing the skin off my heels; my thick leather neck tie was almost choking me. I would have given all I owned to get back into ordinary clothes!" But the high collars and leather neck ties were necessary to prevent the vicious Victorian crime of 'garrotting' – where the criminal crept up behind someone and strangled them.

3. Apart from 'Peeler' the police were called 'Raw Lobsters' – because lobsters have bluish blood rather like the colour of police uniforms – and 'blue devils'. They were also called 'crushers' and 'pigs'.

4. Policemen were being killed on duty within a year of the police force being formed. On 29 June 1830 PC Grantham was kicked to death while he was trying to break up a fight in the street. Three weeks later PC Long was stabbed to death trying to arrest a criminal in the Holy Land. They got no help from the public who stood and watched.

5. Officer Restiaux was lucky to escape with his life in November 1840. He led a group of policemen into the Holy Land to arrest a forger. As they left the house with the forger a crowd gathered and pelted the police with stones. They fled with their prisoner but the mob charged. The leader had a knife. Restiaux wrestled with him and disarmed the man. The police escaped with the forger to the safety of the police station.

6. It wasn't just the poor people who hated the new police forces. The rich people objected to paying the taxes that paid for the law officers. The rich often urged their coachmen to lash out at policemen in the streets as they drove past. Some even drove their coaches straight *at* the police.

7. Earl Waldegrave had a particular dislike for the police.

Once he paid a professional boxer to fight a policeman in London's Piccadilly while crowds of his friends watched. The boxer almost killed PC McKenzie. On another occasion Earl Waldegrave joined with his friend to hold PC Wheatley on the ground while his coach drove over him. PC Wheatley survived, but was too badly injured ever to work again.

8. Policemen worked ten hours a day and walked about thirty-two kilometres on duty. They had no rest days and only one week's holiday a year . . . but they didn't get paid for that week! Apart from the dangers there was also the unpleasantness of the job. One policeman reported finding "A wellington boot on the sea shore . . . with a man's foot inside it"!

9. Birmingham had no police force in 1839. When Chartists began to riot there they sent for the London police. A hundred policemen eventually calmed the troubles. Then sixty policemen were sent back to London – and the Chartists heard that only forty were left in Birmingham. (It wasn't only the police who had spies – the Chartists had them too!) The rioters drove the forty policemen into a yard and trapped them there while they rampaged through the town, burning and stealing. This time it took help from the army to sort out the trouble and free the police.

10. By 1848 the police had won much more respect. On 10th April that year the Chartists had their last great meeting in London. The government appealed for the public to join up as special constables to control the mobs. Very soon 150,000 people became special constables. With so many special policemen to keep an eye on them the Chartists held a quiet meeting. Heavy rain drove them home early and they never recovered from this disappointing event.

So? Would you like to have been a policeman in Victoria's early years?

Several policemen found better jobs . . . they became masters of workhouses!

4. THE FOOD FILE

Pathetic pies

The sort of pie that Ellie ate in the story was a mix of tapioca, onions and potatoes. Mrs Martha Gordon published a book called *Cooking for Working Men's Wives* and gave this recipe:

Ingredients

100g beef dripping, melted
225g onions, sliced
1.6kg potatoes, sliced
75g tapioca
salt and pepper
225g plain flour
1 teaspoon baking powder

Method

Soak the tapioca for an hour in cold water.
Take a quarter of the dripping and put it on the bottom of a pie dish.
Add layers of onion, potato, tapioca, salt and pepper.
Mix the flour, baking powder and the remains of the dripping.
Add water till it makes a smooth dough.
Roll it out and make a smooth lid for the pie.
Bake at gas mark 6 (200°C) for about 70–80 minutes.
You might like to try cooking this just to have the

experience of being poor in Victorian times. But, remember, you can have only one piece of this pie, which has been cut into six pieces. It is washed down with water and will probably be the only thing you eat all day.

Children were taught the value of food at school with this little rhyme . . .

*I must not throw upon the floor
The crust I cannot eat;
For many little hungry ones
Would think it quite a treat.*

*My parents labour very hard
To get me wholesome food;
Then I must never waste a bit
That would do others good.*

*For awful waste makes awful want
And I may live to say,
"Oh! How I wish I had the bread
That I once threw away."*

The song was chanted with hand signs – throwing an imaginary piece of bread, rubbing an empty stomach and so on.

Beastly banquets

While the poor were eating tapioca pie, fighting over bones or chewing on scraps of stale bread, Victoria was living a very different life. The queen never seemed to realise that her poor subjects were starving.

In 1839 she went to a banquet given by the Lord Mayor of London. Compare the food at that banquet with a week's food for a Suffolk farmworker's family. . .

	Lord Mayor's banquet	Robert Crick's family
Number at the table:	570	7
Food:	220 serving bowls of soup	Bread
	45 dishes of shellfish	Potatoes
	2 sides of beef	Tea
	10 sirloins, rumps and ribs of beef	Sugar
		Salt
	50 boiled turkeys with oysters	Butter
	80 pheasants	Cheese
	60 pigeon pies	
	45 decorated hams	
	140 jellies	
	200 ice creams	
	40 dishes of tarts	
	100 pineapples	
	various other dishes	
	Champagnes and wines	
Cost:	Total £8172.25	Total 55p
	£14.33 each	1p a day each

The queen had to attend many banquets, so it is not surprising she was fat, and no one then took exercise as we do today.

Which dinner would you rather have eaten? If you had been a starving slumdweller how would you feel when your fat queen rode past?

5. YOUNG VICTORIAN VILLAINS

The Chartists believed that everyone, poor or rich, had a right to education. Everyone should at least be able to read, write and add up.

The poor were able to go to 'ragged schools' in Victoria's time. The trouble was the children learned more than reading, writing and arithmetic . . . they often learned a lot of Victorian villainy! The criminal children taught the good children how to break the law.

Ralph's story.

Ralph is an intelligent-looking boy. He speaks with a slight stammer but swears that he is determined to tell the truth:

I'm twelve and I've been in prison three times. Once for stealing cigars, once for a piece of cotton and once for some pig's feet to eat. I've been whipped twice. I was at Knightsbridge Ragged School for a year. At ragged school I learned reading, writing, tailoring, shoemaking and cleaning the place as well as church lessons. There were forty or fifty boys at ragged school. We went at nine o'clock left at twelve and went back at two. Between twelve and two I went out with the other boys and we often made up parties to go thieving. We thieved all sorts of things. We taught one another thieving. We liked to teach the very young boys best; they're the bravest and the police don't know them at first. The schoolmaster didn't ever know I stole. Teachers told us not to steal but I thought it was fun. God is a spirit in heaven and he's everywhere.

If I do wrong I shall be burnt in the fire. It frightens me to think of it sometimes. I was first taught to steal by a boy I met at the ragged school. He said, "Come along and I'll show you how to get money." I stole some cigars and the other boy, a little boy, kept watch. I was caught that first time. I'd never have been a thief if it hadn't been for that ragged school, I'm sure I shouldn't.

Ralph was lucky to get away with a whipping in the 1840s. Just a few years before the punishments were much harsher!

✗ In 1801 a boy was sentenced to death for breaking into a house and stealing a spoon. He was thirteen years old.

✗ In 1808 two sisters were sentenced to death for a small theft. They were aged eight and eleven years.

✗ In 1831 a boy was sentenced to death for setting fire to a house. He was nine years old.

✗ In 1833 a boy was sentenced to death for pushing a stick through a cracked shop window and stealing two pence worth of printer's ink. He was nine years old.

These death sentences were later changed to long stretches in prison and beatings.

Miserable masters

Ragged schools were formed wherever there was a space for forty or so children. The Bloomsbury Ragged School was held in a loft over a cowshed!

Richer parents, like John's in the story, could send their sons to public schools or have their own personal teacher. Whichever was chosen a boy could have a hard time. Many teachers really believed that the best way to make a boy learn was to hit him with a stick.

Augustus Hare had lessons at home . . .

I began my lessons after breakfast. At five years of age I was studying English, History, Arithmetic, Geography, German and Latin. There was often a great deal of screaming and crying over the reading and the arithmetic. I never got on well with the reading till my grandmother took it in hand. She sat over me with a ruler and with a series of hearty bangs on the knuckles, she forced my fingers to go the right way.

The public schools were no better. If the teachers didn't beat you then the older boys (prefects) did. Augustus escaped from his gruesome granny only to end up in Harrow public school where . . .

The bullying was terrible in our time. If the little boys could not keep up at football then they were made to cut large thorn sticks from the hedges and flogged with them till the blood ran down their jerseys. I can truly say that I never learned anything useful at Harrow and had little chance of learning anything. Hours and hours were wasted on useless Latin verses. A boy's school education at this time was hopelessly stupid.

Ragged school or public school. Which would you have preferred? But remember – most children had no choice and never went to school.

Did you know . . .?

In the story John described crossing sweepers – boys who kept busy streets clear of horse-droppings, mud and rubbish. Passers-by rewarded them with money and this gave them a poor but honest living. Then, in 1843, street cleaners were appointed in London . . . and the boy sweepers were put out of business. What could they do now for a living? Beg? Or steal?

The boy Cotton

Nowhere was safe from young villains. Not even Victoria's Buckingham Palace. In 1837, when she moved in, the palace was dirty and cold. The chimneys smoked badly and the fires had to be allowed to die down. The queen shivered.

An eleven-year-old sweep called Cotton found it easy to get into the palace. He hid in the chimneys during the day and came out at night to sleep in the beds which he turned black. He once opened a letter addressed to the queen – probably hoping there was money inside.

Cotton quietly stole articles from the palace and no one knew where they had gone. He hid a sword, a book and some glass ink-pots and probably hoped to sell them later. When he found a pair of trousers he wore them!

Cotton was eventually caught. The amazing thing is that he admitted he had lived there, undetected for a whole year!

The boy Jones

At one o'clock in the morning of 2 December 1840 the queen's nurse heard a noise in the queen's sitting room. She called a servant and they found the boy Jones . . . rolled up asleep under a sofa.

He said "I wanted to see how people like you lived. I thought it would make a good book. I've sat on the queen's throne, saw her in the palace and heard her baby screaming. I expect to be treated like a gentleman, if you don't mind. I'm going to be important in this world!"

In fact he ended up in prison and was then sent to join the navy where his behaviour was described as 'good'.

The boy Jones enjoyed *three* spells of life in Buckingham Palace before he was finally sent away.

Life in the palace was certainly better than in the dreaded workhouse.

The wicked workhouses

Girls like Ellie turned to begging because it was better than going into a workhouse. The trick used by Ellie's father in the story – a parent pretending to give money to encourage the rest of a crowd – was known as 'Playing the Noble'. If the child had pretty ringlets and looked ill, so much the better.

Parents often sent their children begging – one London couple made a very good living by sending their four daughters to beg. The girls, aged from five to twelve were sometimes nearly frozen to death. When they were finally stopped, the children were sent off to a workhouse. They would probably have preferred to carry on begging.

The workhouses were usually terrible places to live. People were not supposed to *enjoy* going there – otherwise, the Victorians believed, every tramp would turn up and expect an easy life. If you went into a workhouse . . .

✗ you were split from your family.

✗ You were forced to do hard work like grinding corn, grinding bones or breaking stones. You were also given the job of unpicking old ropes to make 'oakum'. This was used to pack into the joints of wooden ships to stop them leaking. But workhouses were still making their workers unpick oakum when ships were being made of iron.

✗ Your work was paid for with tokens that could only be spent in the workhouse.

✗ Your food was a poor cereal mush called 'gruel' or maybe broth with dry bread or potatoes . . . there wasn't a lot of it and you had to eat it in silence.

✗ Your bed might have been a trough – rather like sleeping in a coffin – or perhaps you'd have had to sleep on the floor. A four-year-old child was punished by being locked in a room full of dead workhouse victims. He had to sleep on their coffin covers.

✗ Your relatives could only visit you with special permission.

✗ You would be punished for breaking the workhouse rules – a boy was flogged so harshly by a workhouse schoolmaster that he died.

✗ Boys were made to do gardening, shoemaking and tailoring while girls did cleaning, laundry and cooking. Teachers were paid to take jobs in the workhouse – the best teachers didn't want to! And when the children were supposed to be having lessons they were often made to dig, sew, do the washing or cooking!

Rules included :

> No speaking during meals.
> Husbands and wives must live apart.
> No beer to be drunk.
> No tobacco to be smoked.
> Everyone capable of working must do so.

So the miserable people who ended up there worked hard and had as little food as they could survive on. Reports described the awful conditions – and storytellers told horrific tales. But storytellers can exaggerate, can't they?

Terrible tales

These are two descriptions of workhouse misery. One is fiction – the other is true. But can you tell which is which?

1. The cannibal

"The room in which the boys were fed was a large stone hall, with a copper [pan] at one end; out of which the master ladled the gruel at meal times. Of this festive composition each boy had one porringer [bowl], and no more – except on occasions of great public rejoicing, when he had two ounces and a quarter [63 grams] of bread besides. The bowls never wanted washing. The boys polished them with their spoons till they shone again; and when they had performed this operation (which never took very long), they would sit staring at the copper with such eager eyes, as if they could have devoured the very bricks of which it was composed; employing themselves, meanwhile, in sucking their fingers with a view of catching any stray splashes of gruel. At last they became so hungry that one boy hinted to his companions that, unless he had another bowl of gruel he was afraid he might happen to eat the boy who slept next to him. He had a wild, hungry eye, and they believed him."

2. The bone pickers

"The bone pickers are the dirtiest of all the inmates of our workhouse; I have seen them take a bone from the dung heap and gnaw it while reeking hot with the process of decay. Bones from which the meat has been cut raw, and which still had thin strips of flesh sticking to them, they scraped carefully with their knives and put the bits, no matter how befouled with dirt, into a wallet or pocket. They have told me that, whether in broth or grilled, they were the most savoury dish that could be imagined. These creatures are often hardly human in appearance, they have no human tastes or understanding, nor even human feelings, for they revelled in the filth which we expect to see in dogs and other lower animals but which to us is sickening."

Answer

Extract 1 is fiction. It is taken from the book *Oliver Twist* by Charles Dickens. Of course Dickens had thousands of readers and they were shocked by the description of workhouse life. The Infant Pauper Asylum in Tooting (near London) housed 1400 children aged two to fifteen. Many died in this harsh workhouse where children had to eat standing up, were beaten and were made to work – the money from their work all went into the pockets of the keeper called Druett. The 'guardians' inspected the place and the children had to pretend to be happy – any child who complained to a guardian was thrashed afterwards. The story of Oliver Twist may have been fiction but it did not exaggerate and it did make people realise a change was needed.

Extract 2 is fact. It is an eyewitness account taken from the *Report on the sanitary condition of the labouring population of Great Britain* by Edwin Chadwick. The bone pickers were usually given piles of old bones from local butchers' shops. Their job was to grind the bones up and put the 'bone meal' into sacks. But when they found strips of meat left on the bones they saw it as a free meal. In 1845 a group of bone pickers in Andover started to fight over the scraps of meat and the fight turned into a full-scale riot in the workhouse. This riot made the government take notice of the workhouse problems and slowly they began to change for the better.

The Starvation Law

People like Charles Dickens tried to change the miserable conditions of the poor by writing stories like *Oliver Twist*. It made the upper classes realise how miserable workhouse life could be.

Not everybody could write as powerfully as Dickens. Some wrote sad poems and sold them as single sheets – pamphlets. The poetry may be terrible but the meaning is clear – 'We hate the upper classes for making the laws that put us into workhouses.'

The New Starvation Law Examined *by Reuben Holder*

If you buy my story and carefully read,
I'm sure it will make the hearts in you bleed.
The lions at London, with their cruel paw,
You know they have passed a starvation law.

To think they should pass such a law in our day
To rob us by stopping a poor widow's pay.
And if they don't like their pay to be stopped
Against their own will in the workhouse they're popped.

There's many a poor child goes ragged and torn
While lords and their horses are fed with best corn.
The poor have hard labour, this is understood,
In handmills the grain they must grind for their food.

The grinding it fills them with great hunger pangs;
Like men in a prison they will work them in gangs.
The master instructs them the law to obey,
The governor makes sure it's all work and no play.

Like the fox in the farmyard they slyly do creep,
These hard-hearted wretches, Oh, how dare they sleep?
I think that they're planning, the whole country o'er
To see what's the worst they can do to the poor.

Poems and stories tried to 'persuade' the rich and powerful to change the laws.

The Chartists used that method – writing in the *Northern Star* newspaper – but they soon realised that writing pamphlets wasn't going to change things very quickly. They wanted more direct action . . .

6. THE EVENTS FILE

Rioting rebels

The Chartists wanted every man in Britain to have a vote for the elections to Parliament. A few even wanted women to have a vote. They didn't always agree on *how* they should make the government take notice of them.

✗ The people of the south thought they should *persuade* the government with peaceful protests – petitions and strikes.

✗ The north agreed . . . but said that if the government didn't listen the Chartists should turn to *violence* even though they knew they would be fighting the police and the army.

✗ O'Connor said, "I am for peace – but if peace does not give us the law then I am for war with the knife."

✗ Chartist Peter Bussey was even more violent, "Every man should own a musket, it should be part of the furniture of his house . . . and he should know how to use it!"

✗ A poster in Manchester declared:

> *Now or never is your time; be sure you do not neglect your weapons. When you do strike let it be with sticks or stones but let the blood of all your enemies moisten the soil of your native land.*

✗ In 1842 a half-starved Chartist cried, "It's better to die by the sword than to die by hunger. And, if we are going to be butchered, why not start the bloody work at once?"

Chartists couldn't agree on the use of violence – but it was never far from their thoughts.

The Newport massacre

Gwent, 4 November 1839

Violence failed at Newport and it failed in the same year at Birmingham. But peaceful petitions had also failed. What was left for the Chartists?

Assassination, perhaps?

Mr Punch's petition

There was more support for the Chartists in the years when prices were high and people went hungry. So the Chartists were popular in really bad years of 1839, in 1842 (when Victoria was attacked three times) and again in 1848.

Sadly the peaceful petitions are what lost the Chartists their final battle. When the 1848 petition went to Parliament Feargus O'Connor said there were six million signatures on it. When they were counted there were fewer than two million. But, worse, the petition included several stupid signatures including:

✗   Queen Victoria
✗   Mr Punch
✗   No Cheese
✗   Sir Robert Peel

Chartism was being treated as a joke.

> *Did you know . . .?*
> Feargus O'Connor hoped to have half a million people on his last great Chartist meeting in 1848. *The Times* newspaper said only 20,000 turned up and it was a failure. O'Connor went insane four years later. When he died in 1855 50,000 turned up at his funeral. If that number had turned up for the 1848 meeting then the Chartists might have won their battle!

7. VICTORIAN WOMEN FILE

Victoria was a woman, yet when she was queen she did nothing to help women in Britain. They were practically owned by their husbands and they stayed that way.

When the women went out to work in factories they were paid far less than men for doing the same job – sometimes less than half – and they had to accept that.

But not all women led quiet and meek lives . . .

Carrotty Kate

George Sanger was a showman with a travelling fair in Victorian times. He told the story of how one week they set up their shows on Lansdown Hill near Bath. Their swings and merry-go-rounds entertained the children while the farmers met and traded their animals; the side-shows and the food stalls made mountains of money and everyone was happy . . . until it grew dark.

From the sickening slums of Bath an army was marching towards the fair. An army of thieves and villains was out to rob the fair. The few police were powerless. This was an organised group led by a wild and powerful hulk . . . and that leader was a woman. A huge, ginger-haired brute known locally as Carrotty Kate from Bull Paunch Alley.

George Sanger was a boy at the time but he could still remember the scene when he wrote about it seventy years later . . .

Carrotty Kate, with her red hair flying wildly behind her, urged the gang of ruffians to wreck the fair. The drinking booths were the first to suffer. The mob took control of them, half-killed some of the unfortunate owners and drank them dry. Then they started to wreck the booths. Canvas was torn to shreds and platforms turned into bonfires. Wagons were battered and overturned, show fronts that had cost a fortune were battered to fragments. Everywhere there was ruin and destruction.

When the gang staggered home in the early hours of the morning the showmen plotted their revenge. Thirty of the strongest, armed with clubs, chased after the gang and succeeded in capturing Carrotty Kate and a dozen of her men. The men were tied together and dragged through a muddy pond at the bottom of Lansdown Hill till they were half drowned. Then they were tied to the wheels of the show carts and whipped with whale-bone whips.

Kate was seized by six strong women and caned till they were exhausted. The giant woman just cursed them before she was allowed to crawl back down the hill and home to her hideous slum.

Miserable miners

In 1842, while Victoria was parading in her carriage above ground, girls and women were struggling to make a living by working under the ground – in coal mines.

Women were used to carry the coal from the coal-face to the surface. They would drag the coal in trucks or carry it in baskets on their shoulders. They often had to climb ladders with the heavy baskets on their backs. In 1842 one twelve-year-old girl had to climb so many ladders that they were higher than St Paul's cathedral!

A thirty-seven-year-old woman described her work dragging coal trucks . . .

I have a belt round my waist and a chain passing between my legs and I go on my hands and feet. The road is very steep and we have to hold on a rope. When there is no rope we just catch hold of whatever we can. The pit is very wet where I work and the water comes over our clog tops always. I have seen it above my knees and it rains in at the roof terribly. My clothes are wet through almost all day long. I have pulled trucks till the belt took the skin off me. The belt and chain is worse when we are expecting a child. My husband has beat me many a time for not being ready on time.

Country comforts

Some people had the idea that living and working in the countryside was healthier than the town slums or easier than the coal mines. Not for the poor. The wages for farmworkers were terrible and life for a labourer's wife as bad as anywhere else. A newspaper reporter described his visit to a cottage in 1849 . . .

The cabin gives the appearance of having been suddenly thrown up out of the ground. The wall seems covered in cold sweat and is fast crumbling to decay. It is so low that your face is practically level with the thatched roof as you enter. There are just two rooms, and the only furniture is a small table, three old chairs and a shelf for a few plates. As you enter a woman rises. She is not as old as she looks for she is careworn and sickly. She has an infant in her arms and three other children are rolling on the floor at her feet. They have nothing on their feet and their clothes are rags and patchwork. They are filthy and the woman whines that she has no way of keeping them clean. In a while another child enters with a few pieces of dry wood which she has picked up. This is not the whole family yet. Two boys and their father have been out at work and they arrive back for dinner. The eldest girl holds the baby while the mother takes a large pot from the fire and pours on to a large dish some potatoes. This with a little bread is their entire meal.

No wonder so many people moved from the country to the factory towns. It couldn't have been worse. Or could it?

Foul factories

An eight-year-old girl was questioned by factory inspectors and talked about working fifteen or sixteen hours a day in 1832. She slept a few hours then hurried back to the factory. Hopefully she'd make it on time . . . or else!

Not all eight-year-old girls worked in the mills. Some were given jobs as 'nurses'. They looked after babies so the mothers could go to work in the mills.

If the babies cried then they could always be drugged with a medicine known as 'Godfrey' or 'Quietness'. This drug put the children to sleep. Unfortunately it also affected the babies' health – they usually grew up weak and sickly.

There were other punishments too for women spinners. They were not beaten but they were given heavy fines. The fines in a Manchester mill were . . .

Any spinner found with a window open	fine – 1 shilling
Any spinner found dirty at work	fine – 1 shilling
Any spinner found washing herself	fine – 1 shilling
Any spinner putting her gas out too soon	fine – 1 shilling
Any spinner using gas in the daylight	fine – 2 shilling
Any spinner found whistling	fine – 1 shilling
Any spinner being five minutes late	fine – 1 shilling
Any spinner being sick and not finding a suitable replacement	fine – 6 shilling

And you thought your school rules were harsh?

Changes . . .

A law passed in 1844 said children of eight to thirteen could work no more than six and a half hours a day. Women were not allowed to work underground in the mines.

A second law of 1847 said women should work no more than ten hours a day. In 1850 it was increased again by half an hour!

In 1870 a law allowed married women to keep the money they earned . . . before that it had belonged to their husbands.

In 1882 women were allowed to own property.

By 1918 women over thirty were finally allowed to vote.

Would you have enjoyed being a woman in Victorian times?

Gruesome guessing

If you were an upper-class person living in Manchester in 1842 then you could expect (on average) to live thirty-eight years. But, if you were in the labouring class how long would you expect to live?

a) 37 years
b) 27 years
c) 17 years

Answer:

c) In London slums like the Holy Land people like Ellie lived, on average, twenty-two years. Upper-class people, like John, lived twice as long – about forty-four years. The unhealthiest place in 1842 was Liverpool. The average death age there was fifteen years old. Queen Victoria lived to be eighty-one.

Part Three
The truth about
the Assassin

31 May 1842

"John Francis wasn't a Chartist," Ellie insisted.

Officer Restiaux had made sure that John Francis was secure and on his way to prison before he returned to us at the roadside.

"He was at the Chartist meeting," he told her.

"So was I!" Ellie said. "So were you, come to that."

Restiaux shook his head. "All right. I'll admit John Francis wasn't sent by O'Connor to kill the queen. But O'Connor's a dangerous man. A madman, if you ask me. He would be pretty pleased to see the queen killed. It's the sort of thing that might scare Parliament into giving way to the Chartists."

I thought of the meeting in that theatre the night before. "He might not send people out to assassinate the queen," I said. "But he stirs up violence. People like John Francis can use that as an excuse to make trouble." Restiaux nodded.

Suddenly I felt a stinging slap on the face and looked in amazement at Ellie. Her eyes were fierce and her voice hissed as she said, "What do you mean 'people like John Francis'? I happen to be people like John Francis. And if *you* lived like *we* do – instead of in your big, posh, clean house with servants to blow your nose and wipe your boots – then *you'd* be angry. *You'd* want things to change, wouldn't you?"

"I . . . I . . . I wouldn't resort to murder," I said primly.

"How do *you* know? Eh? How do you *know*? You don't *understand*, do you? You can come to the Holy Land and curl up your nose at the way we live. You can even feel sorry for us and say you want us to have a better life. But it's only the likes of Feargus O'Connor that'll do anything to try and help us to change. And if Mr O'Connor thinks violence is the way then we'll try it. I tell you one thing . . . John Francis or Bill Bean are worth ten of you and your father," she spat. She turned and walked up the hill and back to the dark streets where she belonged.

Officer Restiaux was as shaken by her outburst as I was. "The politician and author, Benjamin Disraeli, says pretty much the same thing," Restiaux said quietly. "He believes that Victoria reigns over *two* nations, each as ignorant of the other's thoughts and feelings as if they lived on different planets; the two nations have different manners, eat different food and are not governed by the same laws. The two nations? Why, the rich and the poor."

I'd heard the violence in Feargus O'Connor's talk, I'd seen the violence of John Francis' gun and I'd felt the violence of Ellie's slap. It made my teacher's violence seem a small thing.

I wanted to talk to Ellie again. I just wanted to talk to her. I wanted to apologise.

Apologise for being rich.

But I never saw the red-haired girl again. I often wonder what happened to her.

I know Mr O'Connor died a dozen or so years later – he went mad and was locked away.

I know John Francis was sentenced to death but was reprieved and sentenced to a life of hard labour, transported to Tasmania.

I know Prince Albert died within twenty years and grieving Victoria shut herself away from her people for another twenty. Strangely the secret and private widow lived so long that she became popular!

I know that Mr Peel's police force also became popular in time. At first everyone had suspected them of being government spies, but they earned their respect in the following years. Officers like Restiaux were so honest and fearless that we learned in time to trust them and even depend on them.

But I never knew what happened to Ellie Morgan.

Yet, strangely, when Ellie walked away it wasn't quite the end of the story . . .

4 July 1842

Three days after John Francis' second assassination attempt, my father walked into the drawing-room and slapped the evening newspaper on the table. "John! Officer Restiaux is here to see you," he announced.

"I thought I'd finished making my statements to the police," I said.

"No," he said running a finger over the newspaper absently. "No. This is something else. There has been another attempt on the queen's life."

"Another!" I could scarcely believe what I was hearing.

"Don't repeat what I say like some kind of idiot. Another attempt."

"Where?"

Officer Restiaux entered the room and answered my question.

"In the Mall. Her majesty was in a carriage with King Leopold of Belgium when a youth leaped out and fired a pistol at her."

"Was she hurt?" I asked.

Restiaux shook his head. "We recovered the pistol and it seems it was more full of paper and tobacco than powder. Apparently some pathetic creature was trying to copy the actions of John Francis. But he got away. He'll have to be caught and punished or the queen will never be able to ride in public again."

"I see. But why are you telling me? I wasn't there this time!"

"No, but you were at the last attempt. There was a girl with you . . ."

"Ellie," I said.

"And a small, hunch-backed sickly youth."

"I remember," I said carefully.

"He answers the description of the youth who shot at her majesty in the Mall," Restiaux finished.

My mind raced. Bill Bean had tried to kill the queen! Poor Billy. What could he hope to gain? A little fame, perhaps. Just for once, in his miserable life, did he want to be a hero?

"The youth that brought the message to me the other night, John," my father reminded me.

"Ah . . . yes. Ellie knew him."

"Unfortunately Ellie seems to have disappeared," the officer said. "We hoped you could help us by telling us the youth's name."

"His name?" I said and closed my eyes. Finally I said, "The girl never mentioned his name. Sorry I don't know what it is," I lied.

"Sorry, officer, the boy is clearly an idiot," my father snapped.

"The gunman looked pitiful, but we don't believe he was an idiot," Restiaux said.

"Not the gunman. My son. *He's* the idiot," my father said coldly. He never really forgave me. I don't think he ever believed me.

My lie didn't help. The police rounded up all the hunchbacked youths in London and Bill Bean was arrested. He was transported, like John Francis, poor lad.

Things like that affect your life.

I know that, as I grew up, I tried to be a better human being after my adventures with Ellie and the Chartists. I tried to use my wealth and power for the good of others. Perhaps that wasn't enough.

In a strange way I lived my life in the hope of seeing Ellie again. I wanted to tell her that I wasn't as bad as she'd thought at that last bitter meeting. I wanted her to approve of me. I'll never know if she could forgive me for the crime of being born rich.

We lived in two different nations.

EPILOGUE

In all, there were eight attempts on Victoria's life. The first by Edward Oxford in 1840, the three described in this story and four more before she finally died, of old age, in 1901.

All of the characters except John, Ellie and their parents, really existed. Even though John is fictional it is true that a boy witnessed Francis' first attempt and reported it to the palace where Prince Albert agreed that he too had seen a gunman in the crowd.

It was Albert's idea that the queen should allow herself to be a target for a second attempt. Amazingly Sir Robert Peel agreed – though he can't have been very happy about the idea. If the police had failed, then *they* would have been blamed for failing to protect Victoria!

The story has made a link between John Francis and Bill Bean which cannot be proved. But it is likely that Bill Bean attempted what today's police call a 'copy-cat' crime.

What was never made clear was *why* John Francis would have wanted to kill the queen? Was he. . .

- simply jealous of her wealth and power?
- insane? Victoria insisted that he was not 'mad' but 'cunning'.
- angered by the misery of the London slums? He couldn't vote to change it and he couldn't work to change it. All he could do was lash out at the symbol of the powers that ruled the country, Queen Victoria.
- an assassin, employed by Feargus O'Connor to strike a blow for the Chartists? (O'Connor favoured violence, it is true, but he never publicly suggested killing the queen. Then again he wouldn't say it publicly – he'd have been arrested for treason!)
- An assassin – employed by Queen Victoria to shoot at her – and miss? (History is full of stories of unpopular rulers who arranged attempts on their own lives. After the

1840 attempt Victoria gained a lot of sympathy. Did she fix it again and again every time she felt she was losing the support of the people. She certainly had an unusually large number of attempts against her!

• He was a Chartist and believed that he would help the Chartist cause by killing the queen. (The police never linked Francis to the Chartists directly. But there was a great deal of Chartist activity in London at that time and Francis must have been influenced by it.)

So? Why did John Francis shoot at Queen Victoria? He never explained.

We'll never be able to prove any of these ideas. You just have to look at the evidence and decide which is the most likely? What do you think?

It's a true mystery of history.